This edition published in 2002
The Southwestern Company
Nashville, Tennessee

Reprinted 2003

ISBN 0-87197-489-4

Produced by Miles Kelly Publishing Ltd
Bardfield Centre, Great Bardfield, Essex CM7 4SL, UK

Editorial Director: Anne Marshall
Editor: Mark Darling
Copy Editor and Indexer: Lynn Bresler
Proofreader: Margaret Berrill
Senior Designer: Jo Brewer
Designers: Sally Lace, Debbie Meekcoms, Robert Walster
Artwork Commissioning: Lesley Cartlidge
Picture Research: Ruth Boardman, Jennifer Hunt, Liberty Newton
Art Director: Clare Sleven

Color reproduction: DPI Colour, Saffron Walden, Essex, UK

Printed in China

CEO: Ralph Mosley
President: Jerry Heffel
Sales Directors: Fred Prevost, Creig Soeder, Dave Causer, Roy Loftin, Jeff Hawley

Vice President, Marketing: Dan Moore
Project Director: Fiona Greenland
Editorial Director: Mary Cummings
Copy Editor: Carolyn King
Associate Editor: Lisa Fairfax
Production Director: Mark Sloan
Production Coordinator: Powell Ropp
Production Manager: Tom Norvell

Specialist Consultants: Dr Belinda Ashon, Clive Carpenter, Janet Dyson MEd (education consultant), Dr Jim Flegg OBE, Tim Furniss, Steve Parker BSc (Scientific Fellow of the Zoological Society of London), Peter Riley BSc, Cbiol, MIBiol, PGCE, Richard Tames MA MSc
Authors: Anita Ganeri MA (Fellow of the Royal Geographical Society), Neil Morris BA, Clare Oliver, Chris Oxlade BSc, Steve Parker BSc, Philip Steele BA, Brenda Williams
The publishers would also like to thank: Cindy Leaney MA, DTEFLA, CTEFLA

The publishers would like to thank the following artists whose work appears in this book: Mark Bergin, CM Buzer/Studio Galante, Steve Caldwell, Mark Davis, Peter Dennis, Richard Draper, Nicholas Forder, Chris Forsey, Mike Foster/Maltings Partnership, Luigi Galante/Studio Galante, Alan Hancocks, Tony Kenyon, Sue King/SGA, Kevin Maddison, Massimiliano Maugeri/Studio Galante, Debbie Meekcoms, Helen Parsley, Pete Roberts, Martin Sanders, Peter Sarson, Gwen Tourett, Mike White.

The publishers would like to thank the following sources for the use of their photographs in this book:
Corbis: 8, Steve Raymer; 15, Ned Gillette; 18, Tiziana and Gianni Baldizzone; 23, David Turnley; 24–25, Veiga Leal; 26, Roger Ressmeyer; 27; 30, Jonathan Blair. Hutchison: 11, Tony Souter; 20, Nick Haslam. Legoland A/S: 29. Photodisc: 9.

Contents

Who rules the world?

No one! The world is divided into countries, each with its own ruler – a king or queen, a president or general, or perhaps a group of people who rule together as a government. At the moment there are 193 countries in the world, but that number is sure to change. Countries sometimes divide, or join together, to make new countries.

Map numbers

1 *El Salvador*
2 *Honduras*
3 *Panama*
4 *Jamaica*
5 *Puerto Rico*
6 *Dominica*
7 *St. Vincent*
8 *Grenada*
9 *St. Kitts & Nevis*
10 *Antigua & Barbuda*
11 *St. Lucia*
12 *Barbados*
13 *Trinidad & Tobago*
14 *Guyana*
15 *Suriname*
16 *French Guiana*
17 *Estonia*
18 *Denmark*
19 *Latvia*
20 *Lithuania*
21 *Belarus*
22 *Netherlands*
23 *Belgium*
24 *Germany*
25 *Czech Republic*
26 *Slovakia*
27 *Luxembourg*
28 *Switzerland*
29 *Liechtenstein*
30 *Austria*
31 *Hungary*
32 *Moldova*
33 *Slovenia*
34 *Croatia*
35 *Romania*
36 *Andorra*
37 *San Marino*
38 *Bosnia-Herzegovina*
39 *Yugoslavia*
40 *Monaco*
41 *Vatican City*
42 *Albania*
43 *Macedonia*
44 *Georgia*
45 *Armenia*
46 *Azerbaijan*
47 *Turkmenistan*
48 *Uzbekistan*
49 *Kyrgyzstan*
50 *Tajikistan*
51 *Afghanistan*
52 *Cyprus*
53 *Lebanon*
54 *Israel*
55 *Kuwait*
56 *Bahrain*
57 *Qatar*
58 *United Arab Emirates*
59 *Bhutan*
60 *Bangladesh*
61 *Laos*
62 *Cambodia*
63 *Brunei*
64 *Singapore*
65 *Gambia*
66 *Guinea-Bissau*
67 *Burkina Faso*
68 *Benin*
69 *Eritrea*
70 *Ivory Coast*
71 *Ghana*
72 *Central African Republic*
73 *Togo*
74 *Cameroon*
75 *São Tomé & Príncipe*
76 *Equatorial Guinea*
77 *Congo*
78 *Uganda*
79 *Rwanda*
80 *Burundi*
81 *Malawi*
82 *Comoros*
83 *Swaziland*
84 *Lesotho*

Countries and continents

There are nearly 200 countries, but only seven continents. Continents are the huge, main stretches of land on Earth: Africa, Antarctica, Asia, Europe, North America, Oceania, and South America. Only one continent, Antarctica, has no countries on it at all.

National flags

Flags are flown on important occasions, to represent a country and its people. A flag's colors and design often have a special meaning. Japan, which likes to call itself "the land of the rising Sun," has a red Sun on its flag.

Which countries are dripping wet?

Any of the countries in southern Asia during the rainy season! Here it is hot all year-round, but there are two seasons – dry and rainy. When the monsoon winds bring the rains, it really pours down! Most of the time, the rains are good news. They feed farmers' thirsty crops of rice and vegetables. Sometimes, though, too much rain can cause a flood.

 ***The Nile's miles***

The world's longest river is the Nile in Africa. It flows a distance of 6670 kilometers (4145 miles), from Burundi up to the north coast of Egypt, where it empties into the Mediterranean Sea.

Which country is a giant sandbox?

The biggest desert is the Sahara in northern Africa. The Sahara is so huge that it covers parts of many countries. But do not go there to build sand castles. Even if you survived the scorching heat, biting sandstorms would blow away any sand castles you built!

Do you know?

1. Which two countries border Mount Everest?
2. Where is Lake Baikal, the world's deepest freshwater lake?
3. Which country has the most volcanoes?

1. Nepal, China. 2. Russia. 3. Indonesia.

Huge hole

Canada is home to Earth's biggest crater – Sudbury Crater in Ontario. It would take you more than three-and-a-half days of non-stop walking to go around the edge of it.

Is Greenland really green?

No, most of the island is covered in ice. It was given its name by a Viking, Erik the Red, more than 1000 years ago. He hoped the name would cause other Vikings to want to live on the island.

Where can you find a sky bridge?

The Malaysian capital Kuala Lumpur has a see-through "sky bridge" that links the Petronas Twin Towers and gives a dizzying view of the city. It is one of the world's tallest buildings, soaring 452 meters (1483 feet) into the sky. The tallest building is the CN Tower in Toronto, Canada, rising to 553 meters (1815 feet).

City founders

A story says that Rome (in Italy) was founded by twin boys Romulus and Remus who were brought up by a she-wolf.

Where can you visit a real fairytale castle?

Neuschwanstein Castle, in the German Alps, was dreamed up by King Ludwig II of Bavaria. It stands on a huge rock, where it was built between 1869 and 1886. With its towers and turrets, this building became a model for fairytale castles in theme parks around the world.

Feeling pushy?

Rush-hour trains in Tokyo, Japan, are packed. Railworkers called "pushers" use their bare hands to cram in as many travelers as possible.

? True or false

"Big Ben" is the name of a huge bell in London.

Answer: True
It was named after Benjamin Hall, who made the bell in the 1850s. The bell weighs a massive 15 tons and is 2.3 meters (7.5 feet) high. The clock tower in which it lives is also now called Big Ben.

Who feels warm and cozy in felt?

On the grassy plains of Mongolia, herders live in round, felt tents called yurts. These cozy homes are made from layers of animal-hair felt. There is a smoke-hole at the top, and the yurts stay warm even during the cold Mongolian winter. The yurt and everything in it can be packed up to fit on the back of a horse or two when the family wants to move on.

Turf tops

Early settlers of the American Wild West made do with sod houses until they could afford to build permanent homes. To keep the grass on the sod roof neat, some people tethered a goat up there!

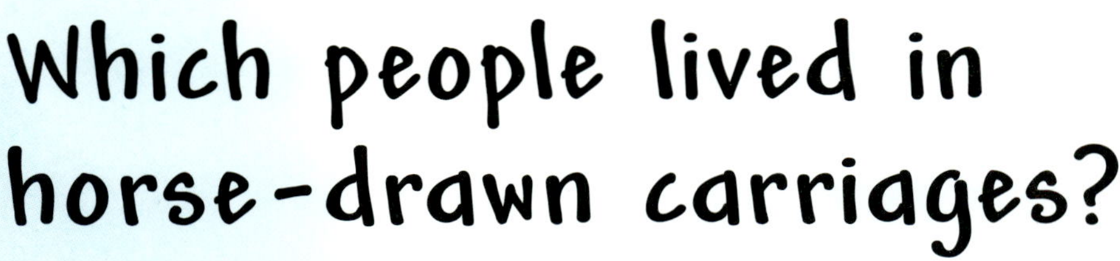

Which people lived in horse-drawn carriages?

The Roma people of Europe, sometimes called gypsies, used to travel around in their own homes, which were beautifully painted and carved wooden wagons. Today, they are more likely to be found living in villages.

On stilts

In the forests of Borneo, groups of families live together in longhouses. These are long buildings raised on stilts, made out of wood and bamboo.

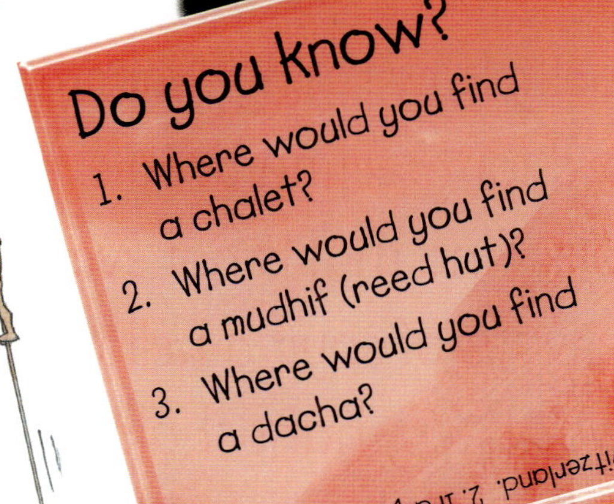

Who will live all over the world?

The people who buy apartments on a giant new ship called *Freedom Ship*. When it is finished, the boat will be like a huge, floating city, carrying around 115,000 people. It will go around the world once every two years, following a route that should always be in the sunshine. The boat will spend most of its time near the world's major cities.

How many ways are there to say hello?

Thousands of ways! There are between 4000 and 7000 different languages spoken in the world today – nobody knows exactly how many. Each has at least one word for greeting people, but usually lots more. And that is not even counting all the ways of saying hello without saying a word – by handshaking, nodding, or kissing, for example!

 **Early words**

Writing began over 6000 years ago. In China, pieces of pottery have been found with marks representing words and numbers.

Why do we not all speak the same language?

There have been lots of attempts to come up with one language that people from every country could speak. One such language is Esperanto. About 100,000 people around the world can already speak it, and about 1000 use it as their main language. The Esperanto for "I love you" is "Mi amas vin."

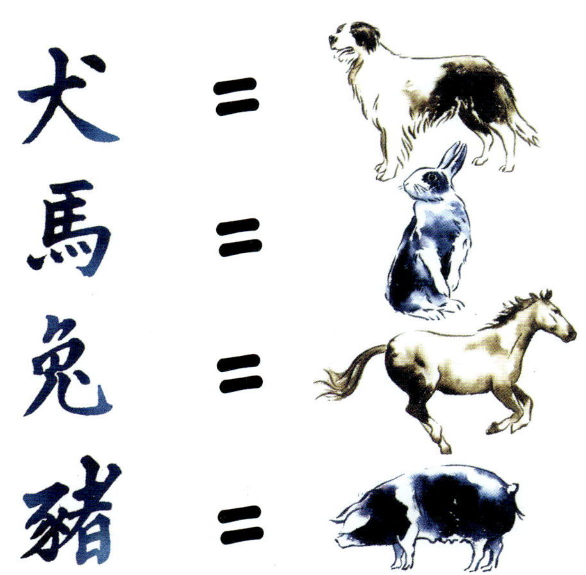

Who writes from top to bottom?

Traditionally, Chinese is written in columns that go from top to bottom, instead of left to right, and it does not use an A-to-Z alphabet like English either. Chinese has picture symbols that stand for whole words. There are more than 40,000 different symbols or characters!

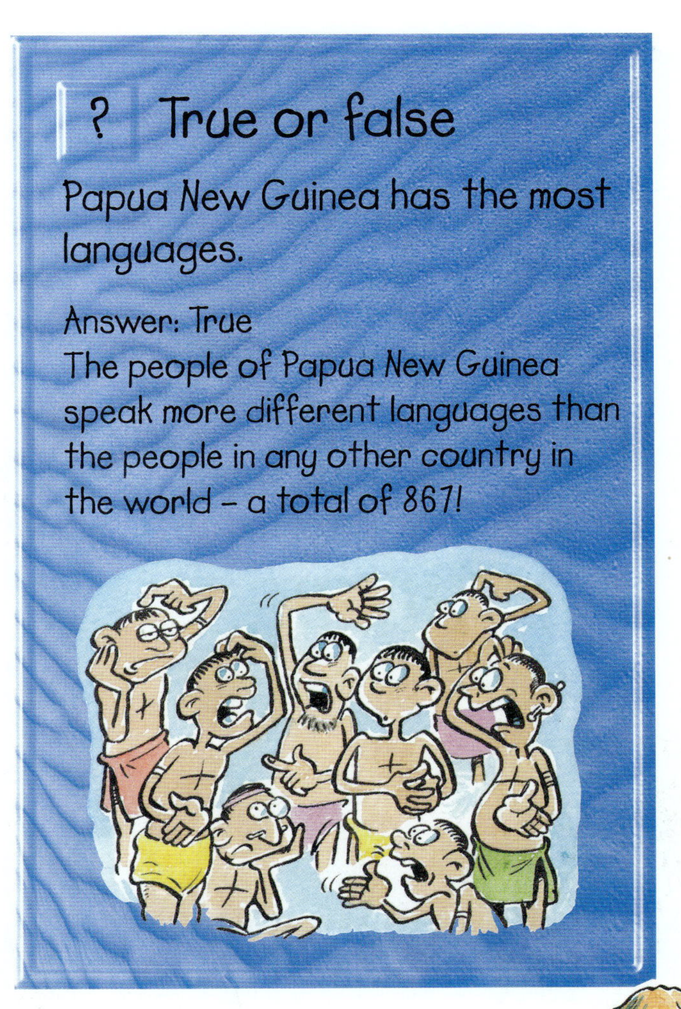

? True or false

Papua New Guinea has the most languages.

Answer: True
The people of Papua New Guinea speak more different languages than the people in any other country in the world – a total of 867!

Who used chocolate for money?

The Aztecs who lived in Mexico around 800 to 500 years ago used cacao beans as money. They used to smash the seeds to make a drink that they called "chocolatl." When Spanish soldiers arrived, they found the drink too bitter for their taste – but they loved it with a spoonful of sugar! Before long, hot chocolate was popular just about everywhere. It was a few hundred years before the solid chocolate bar was invented.

Who chews birds' nests?

In China, bird's nest soup is a treat. It is made from the nests of small birds called swiftlets. It takes brave explorers to find the nests, because swiftlets live high up in remote, pitch-dark caves. The nests, which are made from swiftlets' spit, float like dumplings in the soup.

 **Strange fruit**

The smelliest fruit in the world is the durian fruit that grows in the rainforests of southern Asia. It may stink, but it tastes delicious.

 **Tea terraces**

Tea is made from the leaves of the tea bush, which grows well in tropical parts of the world.

Do you know?

1. Where would you eat gumbo?
2. Where would you eat tagine?
3. Where would you eat goulash?

1. United States. 2. Morocco. 3. Hungary.

Who eats fat, white worms?

One of the favorite snacks of the Aboriginals of Australia used to be the wichety grub. This fat, white worm is sometimes still eaten raw or cooked and is said to taste like nuts. Insects, rodents, and lizards are also a popular treat.

Who fishes with fire and birds?

Japanese and Chinese fishermen use birds called cormorants to dive for fish and bring them to the surface in their beaks. They attract the fish to the water around their boats by lighting fire baskets, and the curious fish swim close to find out what the light is. Then the birds strike. They are put on a long leash in case they decide to try and fly away!

Weed farms

Farmers grow seaweed off the coasts of Indonesia. From the air, their "fields" look like a giant patchwork quilt of reds, browns, and greens.

Wool world

In Australia, sheep outnumber people eight to one. Each sheep produces around 7 kilograms (15 pounds) of raw wool a year. There are nearly 150 million sheep.

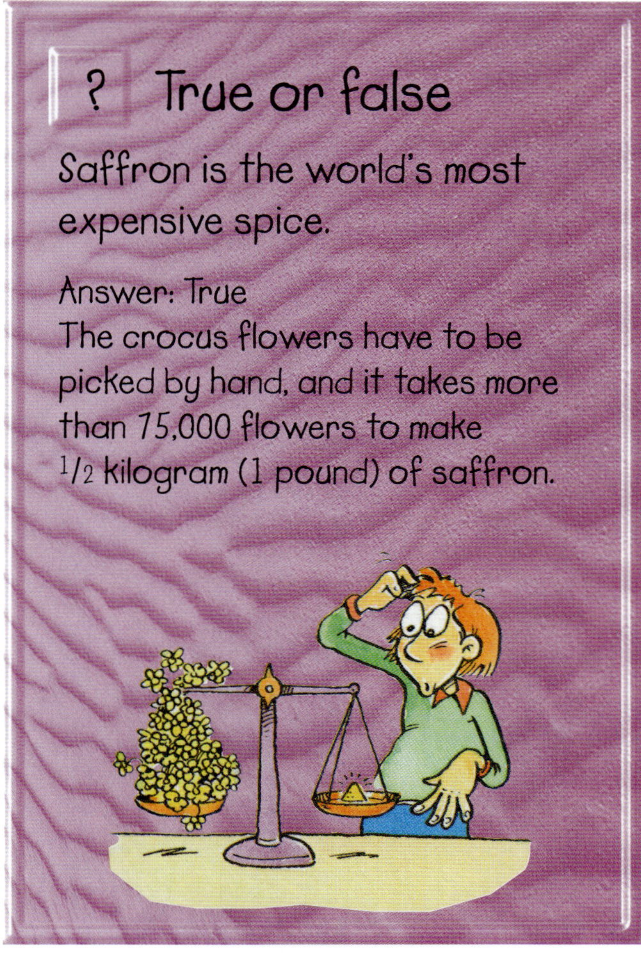

? True or false

Saffron is the world's most expensive spice.

Answer: True
The crocus flowers have to be picked by hand, and it takes more than 75,000 flowers to make 1/2 kilogram (1 pound) of saffron.

Does all milk come from cows?

No. Cow's milk is not the only milk. Around the world, people milk lots of other animals, including goats, reindeer, and yaks. You can also drink plant (soya) milk.

Where do men wear blue veils?

The Tuareg people of the Sahara are known to their desert neighbors as the "Blue People." They are nomads, moving from place to place, herding camels and cattle. Tuareg men dress in blue or white robes and turbans. From the age of 25, they also wear a veil that covers everything but their eyes. It prevents sand from getting in their noses and mouths and protects them from the Sun.

Breezy kameez

In many countries in southern Asia, people wear a loose-fitting tunic over a pair of baggy pants. This outfit, called shalwar-kameez, is popular with girls and boys, men, and women.

Who wears beautiful soft sweaters?

The South American Indians who live in the Andes Mountains knit beautiful sweaters and ponchos out of silky soft alpaca wool. Alpaca are animals related to camels and llamas. They are able to survive the extremes of hot and cold in the Andes. Their long hair is sheared every other year and spun into yarn. This is dyed in bright colors.

Bear necessities

The Inuit, Yakut, and other peoples who live in the Arctic Circle use sealskin, reindeer hides, and polar-bear fur to make cozy boots, leggings, gloves, and hooded parkas.

Do you know?

1. Who wears a dishdash – a long robe?
2. Who wears a kimono – a wrap?
3. Who wears a tartan kilt – a kind of skirt?

1. Arab men. 2. Japanese women. 3. Scottish men.

Who wore chewed shoes?

Many years ago, Native Americans wore soft shoes called moccasins, which were made from deerskin. To make the leather extra soft, the women would chew it for days on end. Stitched from just two pieces of leather, the shoes were then decorated with embroidery or beads.

Which bride paints on gloves and socks?

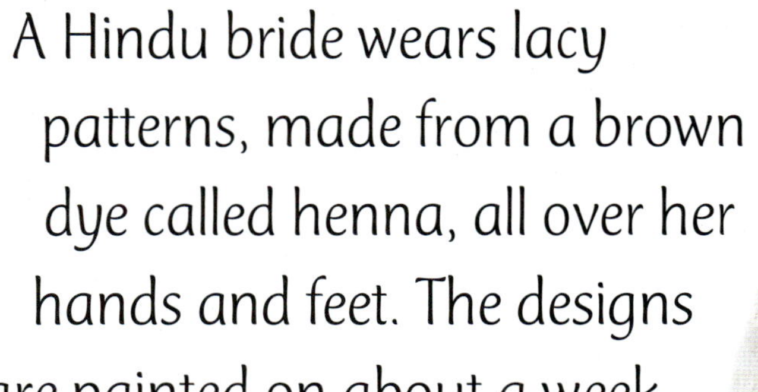

A Hindu bride wears lacy patterns, made from a brown dye called henna, all over her hands and feet. The designs are painted on about a week before the wedding, at a special party. On the wedding day, the bride often wears a red and gold sari and the groom wears a gold turban. These are lucky colors. The couple give each other garlands of flowers, before taking seven steps together around a holy fire.

Who buries their dead in a sports car?

In Ghana, some rich people are buried in the most amazing coffins, carved into fantastic shapes and then brightly painted. Some look like vehicles, such as sports cars, trucks, canoes, and planes. Others are made into animals, such as elephants and eagles.

Where do songs grow up?

Sami parents often give their newborn baby a special made-up song, called a joik. As time passes, the children and their parents and friends add to the song. A joik mixes together different sounds that have a special meaning for the person it belongs to. Sometimes, it is sung along to the beat of a reindeer-skin drum. The Sami people live in Europe – in Norway and Finland.

? True or false

Ghanaians traditionally wear black to a funeral.

Answer: False
Black can be worn as a sign of respect for the dead in many countries, but not all. In Ghana, many mourners wear clothes with red and orange in them.

Sugar skulls

The Mexicans remember dead relatives on the Day of the Dead. They visit the family tomb and decorate it with bright orange marigolds. They eat candy shaped like flowers – and even skulls!

Where can you find the world's holiest city?

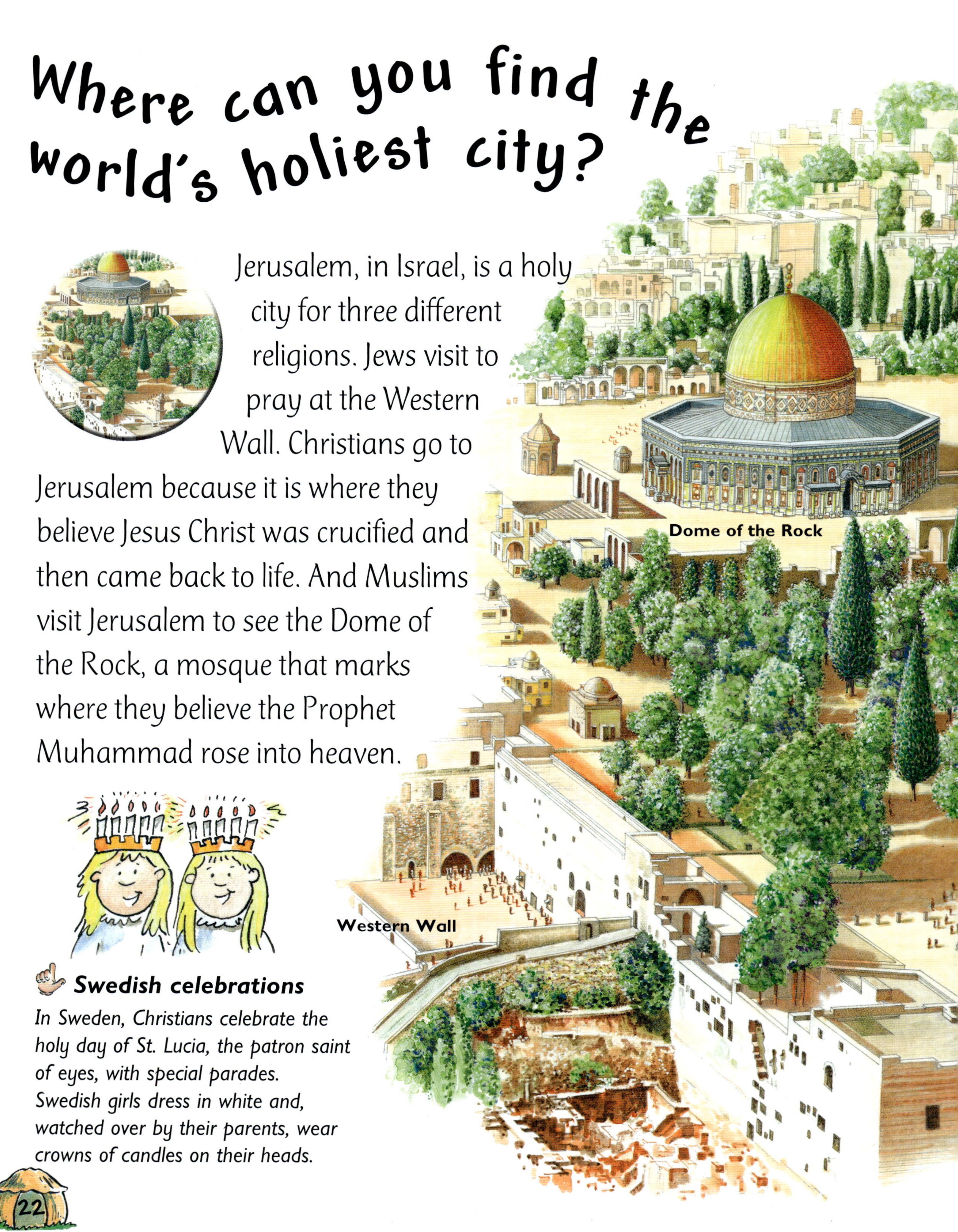

Jerusalem, in Israel, is a holy city for three different religions. Jews visit to pray at the Western Wall. Christians go to Jerusalem because it is where they believe Jesus Christ was crucified and then came back to life. And Muslims visit Jerusalem to see the Dome of the Rock, a mosque that marks where they believe the Prophet Muhammad rose into heaven.

Swedish celebrations

In Sweden, Christians celebrate the holy day of St. Lucia, the patron saint of eyes, with special parades. Swedish girls dress in white and, watched over by their parents, wear crowns of candles on their heads.

Who always prays facing in the same direction?

Wherever they are in the world, all Muslims face the same way when they pray to Allah (God). They face Mecca, in Saudi Arabia, the holy city where the Prophet Muhammad was born. Muslim places of worship, called mosques, all have a pointer on the wall so worshipers know which way to kneel.

Sikh sign

Sikh boys and men never cut their hair. It is one of the signs that they belong to the people who follow the Sikh religion.

Do you know?

1. Which river is sacred to Hindus?
2. Which tree is sacred to Buddhists?
3. Which rock is sacred to Aboriginals?

1. Ganges. 2. Bo tree. 3. Uluru (Ayers Rock).

Who throws powder and water?

At the springtime festival of Holi, Hindus in northern India and Nepal have a lot of fun squirting each other with water and colored powders. One explanation of the meaning of the festival is that Holi tried to burn a good man called Prahlad but in the end she was burned instead. Hindus still light bonfires at Holi, but their favorite part is the messy powder-throwing!

Where is the world's biggest party?

Río de Janeiro, in Brazil, puts on an amazing Carnival every spring. It is just before the period of Lent, when some Christians do not eat rich foods for more than a month. There are lots of street parties, where samba dancers wear sequin-covered costumes and perform for thousands of onlookers.

Who has dragon parades?

Chinese people, who dance through the streets with multi-colored dragons to keep away evil spirits. Of course, they are not real dragons – they are long, snaky costumes with lots of people underneath!

When do elephants dress up?

Each July or August, Buddhists in Sri Lanka celebrate the Buddha's life with a festival, Esala Perahera. On the last night, there is a procession of acrobats, dancers – and over 100 elephants! Each animal wears a coat of silk or velvet, decorated with jewels, and candles or little lightbulbs.

? True or false

The Chinese invented fireworks.

Answer: True
Fireworks or firecrackers are an important part of many celebrations. They were first invented by the ancient Chinese.

Flying fish

Children's Day in Japan is celebrated on May 5. People fly colorful kites shaped like carp fish. Real carp swim upstream in rivers – the kites represent people's hard journey through life.

Where do dancers stamp their feet?

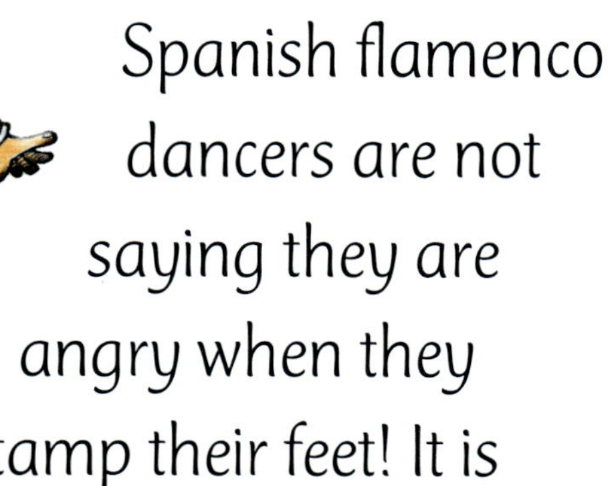

Spanish flamenco dancers are not saying they are angry when they stamp their feet! It is just part of the dance. Flamenco is often danced in pairs, with the man dressed all in black and the woman in a frilled dress. Some dancers click castanets as they whirl and twirl.

Dancing belly

Belly dancing has been popular entertainment since the days of the ancient Egyptians. Often, the dancer's belly button is decorated with a sparkling jewel.

Which actors always quarrel on stage?

The main puppet stars in a Punch and Judy show! These shows have been run in England for hundreds of years. They are performed at the seaside, from a striped booth that hides the puppeteer. As well as grumpy Mr. Punch and his wife Judy, other stars include a crocodile, a dog, and a policeman.

Hollywood, Bollywood

Many of the world's most famous movies are made in Hollywood, in the United States – but even more movies are made in Bollywood! This is the nickname for the Indian city of Bombay, where studios make more than 800 movies each year.

Do you know?

1. Where would you hear a didgeridoo?
2. Where would you hear an alpenhorn?
3. Where would you hear the tabla?

1. Australia. 2. Switzerland. 3. India.

Who goes dotty for bark?

Traditionally, Aboriginals of Australia paint magical pictures on anything – it might be a piece of bark, a stone, or even a wall. The artists mix up natural colors, mostly browns and reds, and use their fingers to pattern their pictures with dots. The pictures are about the time before people were on Earth, which the Aboriginals call the Dreamtime.

Who are the heaviest wrestlers?

Sumo wrestlers in Japan weigh at least 160 kilograms (350 pounds) – more than twice as much as ordinary men. They even have to go on a special diet to keep their weight up. Power is everything as a wrestler tries to make his opponent touch the ground with anything but the soles of his feet, or step out of the ring. Most contests are over in a matter of seconds!

Where can you see plastic animals?

One of the most popular toys in the world is Lego. Its name comes from the Danish phrase "leg godt," meaning "play well." At the Legoland Adventure Park near Billund, Denmark, you can see over 50 million little plastic bricks that have been used to build miniature models of cars and safari animals.

? True or false

The first basketball nets were old shrimping nets.

Answer: False
Basketball was invented in the United States over 100 years ago. The first game was played using two old peach baskets!

Surf's up

Riding the waves on a surfboard for fun dates back hundreds of years. It was probably invented by the people on the Hawaiian island of Maui, in the Pacific Ocean.

Do we know who first won the Olympics?

The ancient Greeks used to hold sports competitions, including a famous one at Olympia in honor of their god Zeus. There is no record of the winners' names, but we know there was running, boxing, and chariot racing. In 1896, the first modern Olympic Games were held in Athens, Greece.

Who gets carried away by dogs?

Traveling around in the icy Arctic is not easy. The traditional way for people to get around was in a sled pulled by dogs. Some Arctic peoples, such as the Sami, used reindeer to pull their sleighs instead. These days, most people prefer snowmobiles, and dogsled racing is more for fun.

Bright bus

In Pakistan, bus drivers paint their vehicles bright colors and decorate them with flowers.

Where do boats go up in an elevator?

At St. Louis Arzviller in France, a canal boat elevator has replaced 17 locks. Before the elevator, it took boats all day to get through the locks and up the slope. Now, the elevator carries them up 45 meters (150 feet) in less than five minutes!

Where can you ride bikes for free?

In the Netherlands, cities provide free bikes. This is to help cut down on the number of people using smelly polluting cars. There are bike "stations" in the city where people can borrow bikes.

Airmail

Some farms in Australia and Africa are so remote that there is no daily postal service. The mail comes by plane once a week, or even once a month!

Do you know?

1. Which canal boat is used in Venice, Italy?
2. Is a junk a truck or a boat?
3. Where would you ride on a bullet train?

1. gondola. 2. boat 3. Japan.

Index